Version 01

La Belle Dame sans Merci

♩ = 130

Original words by John Keats
Music & Arrangement by Jonathan K. Hale

Intro (Ac. Guitar)

let ring- - - - - - - - - - - - - - - -| let ring- - - - - - - - - - - - - - - -|

Verse

what can ail thee, gal lant knight, Alone and pale ly loi te ring?_

X 10

The sedge has wi thered from__ the__ lake, and__ no__ birds sing.

Outro (Ac. Guitar)

legato *f*

2

O what can ail thee, gallant knight,
Alone and palely loitering?
The sedge has withered from the lake,
And no birds sing.

O what can ail thee, knight-at-arms,
So haggard and so woe-begone?
The squirrel's granary is full,
And the harvest's done.

I met a lady in the meads,
Full beautiful-a faery's child,
Her hair was long, her foot was light,
And her eyes were wild.

I placed her on my pacing steed,
And nothing else saw all day long,
For sidelong she would bend and sing
A faery's song.

She found me roots of relish sweet,
And honey wild, and manna-dew,
And sure in language strange she said-
'I love thee true'.

She took me to her Elfin grot,
And there she wept and sighed full sore,
And there I closed her wild sad eyes
With kisses four.

And there she lullèd me asleep,
And there I dreamed-Oh! woe betide!-
The latest dream I ever did dream
On the cold hill side.

I saw pale kings and princes too,
Pale warriors, death-pale were they all;
They cried-'La Belle Dame sans Merci
Hath thee in thrall!'

I saw their starved lips in the gloam,
With horrid warning gapèd wide,
And I awoke and found me here,
On the cold hill's side.

And that is why I sojourn here,
Alone and palely loitering,
Though sedge is withered from the lake,
And no birds sing.

3

Get in the Sailboat

♩ = 93

Words & Music by Alvin H. Hale
Arranged by Jonathan K. Hale

Intro (Ac. Guitar)

Verse (1-3)

There was a time when on this old earth I tra veled on through trou ble and mirth
Oh sin ner friend don't you li sten just now some one to help you make him your vow
We're on our way to hea ven a bove fly ing a lone like a hea ven ly dove

but Je sus came and be ckoned you see get in the sail boat with me.
make up your mind, a ccept him my friend get in the sail boat with him.
Je sus is co ming, co ming a gain get in the sail boat with him.

Chorus

Get in the sail boat with Je_____ sus get in the sail boat with him.

we're travel ling down life's ri ver of time get in the sail boat with

D.S. x 3 al Coda

⊕ Coda

him. we're travel ling down life's

riten. **Fine**

ri ver of time get in the sail boat with him.

Something to build

♩ = 88

Words & Music by Jonathan K. Hale

Chorus

E   B   A   E   B

Some thing to build the me mo ries___ on___ Some thing to keep you warm when the

C#m   A   F#m   B   E

nights are cold and long_____ Oh, ba by___ some thing to build the me mories on.

Verse (1-2)

E   B   C#m   E   B   A

No bo dy said love was ea sy___ but you live and you___ learn___
No bo dy said life was e ven___ what you give and what you get_____

F#m   C#m

You'll make mi sta___ kes but tha's the chance_ you take
can't take back what we___ said can't take back what we did

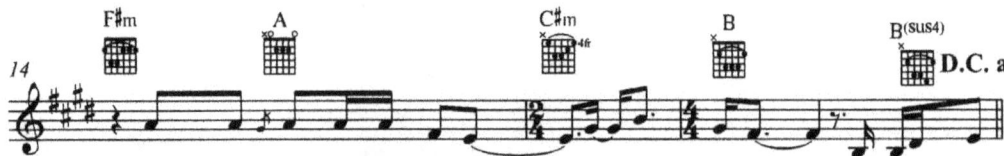

F#m   A   C#m   B   B(sus4)   **D.C. al Fine**

you can't take fire in your heart and_____ not_ get burned___ if___ you want.
but you find some times what you still forgive_____what you can't forget._____

Bridge

17 How can you see in side until you_____ put a way your pride__

20 see what's in our hearts_ and_____ see what's in our minds_ there's

22 beau ty that_ we all hold wi thin_____

24 you walk much bet ter now_ my_____ friend_ cuz you got_

Chorus

26 __ Some thing to build the me_mo ries_ on_ Some thing to keep you warm when the

riten.

29 nights are cold and long_____ Oh, ba_by_ some thing to build the me_ mories on.

Fine

Cold winds

Words & Music by Jonathan K. Hale
Arranged by Jonathan K. Hale

♩=114

Intro (Ac. Guitar)

Verse (1)

I feel a

cold breeze blow and the whispe ring___wind is like dri fting snow___ on a mou ntain___

with the sun light_ still on my skin_

Chorus

And,

oh_____ that'swere I wan na be___ if you would on___ ly close your eyes then *rit.*

2

20 F#m   C#m   **Verse (2)**   F#m   E

you could see what I can see.   *accel.* And I see waves crash ing on the_ docks like

24 Bm   F#m   D   E F#m   E

lost hopes_ dashed up on the_ rocks   but the clouds they_ look so soft_

28 D   E   F#m   E D   E   F#m

so what if we   fall____

31 E D   E   F#m   **Chorus**

And,

34 F#m   C#m   Bm

oh_____ that'swere I wan na be___   if you would on__ ly close your eyes then

37 F#m   C#m   **Verse (3)**   F#m   E

you could see what I can see.   *accel..* And I hear sea gualls cry_ as theysoar so_ high
rit.. - - - - - - -   © 1994 - 2015 Chimery Chimes

9

only_ ea_gles are supposed to_ fly_   but I see you walk a way on the   shore

as   I wave good bye____

Bridge

So let the

cold   winds   wail_____ let the cold wind howl   as they fill my   sails

and roll a cross my   bow   Let the cold winds   bow.

Outro

And I see you walk a way on the   shore__   and I don't know why__

4

but I can't stop it____ a ny more____ so I just wave good bye__

I____ just wave good bye____ I____ just wave good bye.

rit.. - - -

Outro (Ac. Guitar)

rit.. - - -

At this moment

Words & Music by Jonathan K. Hale
Arranged by Jonathan K. Hale

♩ = 140

Intro (Ac. Guitar)

Verse (1-2)

Stu mb ling in the dark   tears fal ling from the sky   try ing to   find my wa y___
Now run ning out of time   I could n't read your mind   still I take all of the bla me___

cir cl ing   in   your   light   will   the   sun   e   ver   rise
they say that   what's done   is   done   so   are   you   glad   you   won?

why   can't   I   live   in   your   da   y?___
I'll   ne   ver   be   the   sa___   me___

Chorus

At this mo   ment   I   love you with all   my   heart___

12

2

At this mo ment you took it just a lit tle too far____ at this mo

ment she said, "I love you with all my heart____

but to mor row mor__ ning__ oh you won't be back no more____ no! no__

Intro (Ac. Guitar)

Bridge

It's hard to hold on when all hope is gone____ but I'm gon na fight__

left here to die but the strong will__ sur vi____ ve__

no, I won't go down___ At this mo

ment___ I love you with all my heart_____

At this mo ment you took it just a lit tle too far_____

at this mo ment she said,"I love you with all my heart_____

but to mor row mor___ ning_ oh you won't be back no more_____ no no___

Outro (Ac. Guitar)

14

4

molto rit. - - - - - - - - - - - - -

This house

Words & Music by Jonathan K. Hale
Arranged by Jonathan K. Hale

♩ = 125

Intro (Ac. Guitar)

Verse (1-2)

When   I   woke up this mor   ning I   knew you were gone   but I
Now when I   close my___ eyes I re a   lize the___ truth   but I

dreamed___ last night I held you   in my arms   I   know I have your pi cture but it's
dream at___ night I'm ly ing   next to you   I   try to play the game but it's just

not e nough   this house is   not   a   home___ with out your lo ve.
no___ use   my life is   not   the   same___ it's all   a ru se.

2

Intro (Ac. Guitar)

Chorus

house is not a ho___ me   and my life is not my own_____   and I

can't go on a lone___with out your lo ve.

Intro (Ac. Guitar)

And this

Verse (3)

Do you know what is like to heed__ the call

on ly to find your self ta king a fall I'm sen ding out a mes sage but there's

__ no re ply and I can't go on with out__ you by my si de.

Intro (Ac. Guitar)

18

4

Chorus

house is not a ho____ me and my life is not my own

____ and I can't go on a lone____ with out your lo ve.

Outro (Ac. Guitar)

Copyright © 1994 -2015 Chimery Chimes

rall. - - - - -

19

Castles

$\quad \downarrow = 87$

Words & Music by Jonathan K. Hale
Arranged by Jonathan K. Hale

Intro (Ac. Guitar)

Verse (1-3)

Are your cast les in the air?   or___ do you e ven
Are your cast les made of stone?   and will you leave me all a
Are your cast les made of steel?   can your heart no lon ger

care?   Will you stand or will you fall?   or___
lone?   Can you fill these em pty halls?   or is the
feel?   Will you keep me han ging on   af ter

2

do you care at all? Cast les in the air.
wri ting on the walls? Cast les made of stone.
love is dead and gone? Cast les made of steel.

let ring- -

Bridge

D.S. al Coda

let ring- ⌐

And all I'll e ver be___ just

crum bles in my_ hands   is washed in to the_ sea___ like cast les   cast les made of

Outro (Ac. Guitar)

sand.

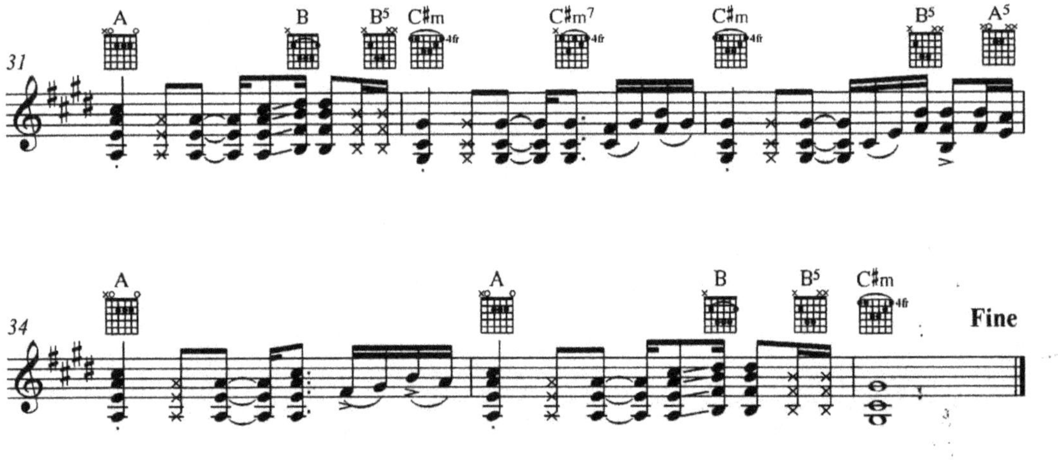
31
A
B
B5
C#m
C#m7
C#m
B5
A5
34
A
A
B
B5
C#m
Fine

Bright side

♩=116

Words & Music by Jonathan K. Hale
Arranged by Jonathan K. Hale

Intro (Ac. Guitar)

Verse (1-3)

Time is wa_
Wind is blow
Rain is fal_

_ sting
_ ing
_ ling

on the bright side of town_
through my win dow now
on the dark side of town_

but there really ain't no rea___ son
and_ no way of know_ ing
but there really ain't no rea___ son

for me to be fee
which way she's go_
for me to be fee

_ling down
_ing now
_ling down

time is wa_sting
wind is blow_ing
rain is fal_ling

on the bright side of town
through my win
on the dark side of town

2

but there really ain't no rea_____ son_____
dow now.
and_____ no way of know_____ ing_____
but there really ain't no rea_____ son_____

for me to be fee_____ ling down
which way she's go_____ ing now
for me to be fee_____ ling down

just be cause the sun
guess I'll just hold

To Coda

D.C. al Coda **Coda**

_____ don't shine on my bright side of town.
_____ on for a new da y now

cause just I'll move_ on

yeah, I'll just move_ on

I'll just move_ on to that bright side of town.

Outro (Ac. Guitar)

Fine

molto rall. _ _ _ _ _ _ _ _

Just cause

♩ = 129

Words & Music by Jonathan K. Hale
Arranged by Jonathan K. Hale

Intro (Ac. Guitar)

E F# G#m E F# B B(SUS4) B

Verse (1-2)

G#m E B F# G#m E F# F#(SUS4) F#

Just be cause you gave up on me____ do I have to give up on you____
Just be cause you left me be hind____ does it mean I won't be a round?____

G#m E B F#

just be cause the sun don't shine____
just be cause you've raised up a wall____

G#m E F# F#(SUS4) F#

To Coda

does it mean the rain falls, too?____
does it mean I can't tear it down____

Chorus

E F# G#m E F# G#m

Of all the things that I don't know___ one thing I can say for sure___

E F# G#m E F# B B(SUS4) B

D.S. al Cod

I'm still in love. I'm still in love I'm still in love with you___

2

Bridge

21

Just be cause you lose the bat tle does it mean you've lost the war?__

25

just be cause you fall from the sad dle does it mean you'll ride no

28

more?

Verse (3)

32

Just be cause there's no thing to say__ does it mean that we can't talk?__

36

and just be cause I don't hold the key____ a ny more

38

does it mean I can't break the lock?__

Chorus

40

Of all the things that I don't know__ one thing I can say for sure__

Fine

I'm still in love. I'm still in love I'm still in love with you___

I'm still in love I'm still in love I'm still in love with you___

Train song

♩ = 137

Words & Music by Jonathan K. Hale
Arranged by Jonathan K. Hale

Intro (Ac. Guitar)

Verse (1)

I said now the time has come for me to be gone

but I don't wan na go a lone

Chorus

What do you do whrn the train keeps rol ling and you wan na get off?

What do you do whrn the rain keeps fal ling

and it just won't stop?

28

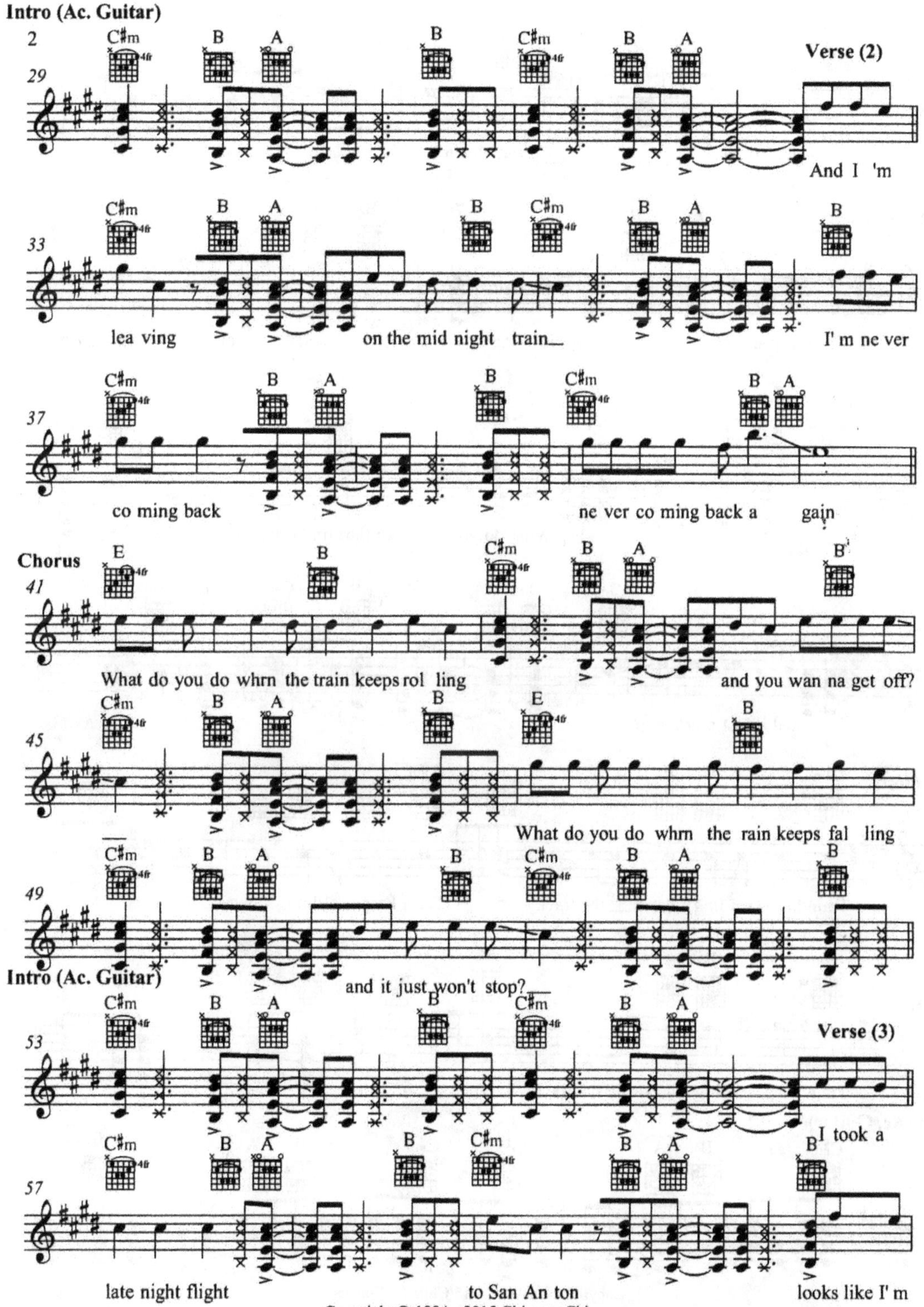
Intro (Ac. Guitar)
Verse (2)
And I 'm
lea ving on the mid night train
I' m ne ver
co ming back
ne ver co ming back a gain
Chorus
What do you do whrn the train keeps rol ling
and you wan na get off?
What do you do whrn the rain keeps fal ling
and it just won't stop?
Intro (Ac. Guitar)
Verse (3)
I took a
late night flight
to San An ton
looks like I' m

hea ded south way down to Me xi co

Chorus What do you do whrn the train keeps rol ling and you wan na get off?

What do you do whrn the rain keeps fal ling

and it just won't stop?

Outro Train keeps rol ling down the track Train keeps rol ling down the track

Train keeps rol ling down the track

Outro (Ac. Guitar)

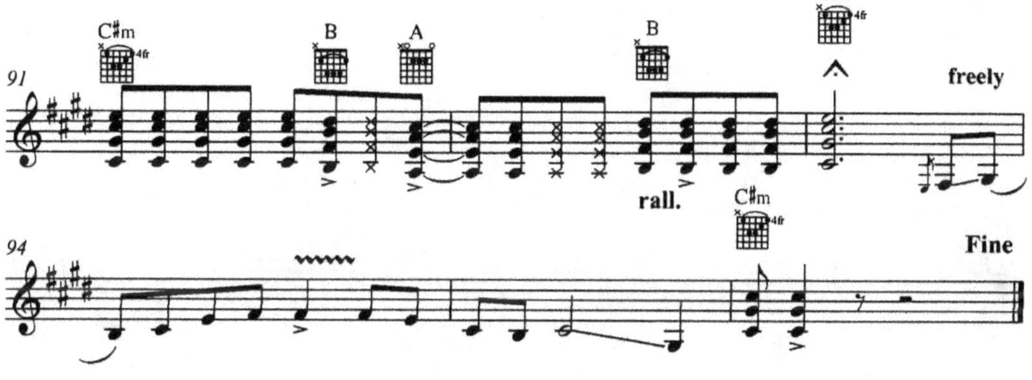
91
C♯m
B
A
B
C♯m
freely
rall.
94
C♯m
Fine

Song of Solomon

♩ = 129

Words & Music by Jonathan K. Hale
Arranged by Jonathan K. Hale

Intro (Ac. Guitar)

let ring---------| let ring---| let ring------| let ring---------|

let ring--| let ring-----| let ring-| A no ther slee pless night and he'd

climbed these ci ty walls   to see her fa ce   but light ning ne ver strikes the same

Verse (1)

Pre-Chorus (1-2)

place twice   till the   sha dows flee and the   dawn_ breaks   So he's
she's

sear ching in_ the ci   ty   in the streets and in_ the square he'll hold her so_ close ne ver
she'll   him

let her go_____   when he finds her there_
him   she him

Chorus

For lo ve is strong as death   jea lou sy cruel as the grave_

its coals are coals of fi_____ re_____   the most ve he me_ nt flames

Intro (Ac. Guitar)

let ring----------   let ring---   let ring-------   let ring-----------

let ring----   let ring-------   let ring--   **Verse (2)** She wakes from a dream   he's

out side it seems_   and she can hear him knoc king   but she's

wai ted too long   and now he's gone   and she's a fraid she's lost__ him.

Intro (Ac. Guitar)

Coda

let ring--------   let ring---   let ring-----   let ring-------   let ring--

Copyright © 1994 -2015 Chimery Chimes

Many wa ters can not quench love

nor can floods drown it____ if a man gave all he had for love

Pre-Chorus (3)

con tempt is all he'd get But I'm sear ching in___ the ci ty

in the streets and in___ the square I'll hold you so___close ne ver let you go____

Chorus

if I find you there____ For lo ve is strong as death

jea lou sy cruel as the grave___ its coals are coals of fi____ re

Freely

Fine

the most ve he me_nt flames____

Cut me out

♩ = 116

Words & Music by Alvin H. Hale
Arranged by Jonathan K. Hale

Intro (Ac. Guitar)

Verse (1-2)

When you were young and love ly___ and your
There are so ma___ ny o thers now that you

heart it beat___ for me   I fell in___ love_with you, dar ling   but it
don't have time for me   so I'll step_ aside___ my true love   and_

end ed_ bitt ter ly   **Chorus** So cut me___ out_ of your pi cture and
give you_ your li ber ty

take it and_ throw it a way   cut me   out_ of your

2

E   C#m   B   E

22

pic ture   but_ I'll re_____ turn some_ day

Intro (Ac. Guitar)

C#m B5 B B(sus4)   B5 C#m   C#5 A A5 C#m   B5 B B(sus4)   B5 E E(sus4)

25

Oh_____   oh_____   oh_____   oh____

E   E(sus4)   **Chorus** E   A

32   **D.S. al Fine**

_   Cut me_ out_ of your pic ture   and take it and throw it a

E   A   E   C#m B   E

36

way   cut me out_ of your pic ture   but I'll re____turn some day

Intro (Ac. Guitar)

C#m B5 B B(sus4)   B5 C#m   C#5 A A5 C#m   B5 B B(sus4)   B5 E E(sus4)

41

Oh_____   oh_____   oh_____   oh____

E   E(sus4)   C#m B5   B B(sus4)   B5 C#m   C#5 A A5

48

_   Oh, I'll_____ re turn   I'll_____ re turn

C#m B5   B B(sus4)   B5 E E(sus4)   E   E(sus4)

53

I'll_____ re turn   some day

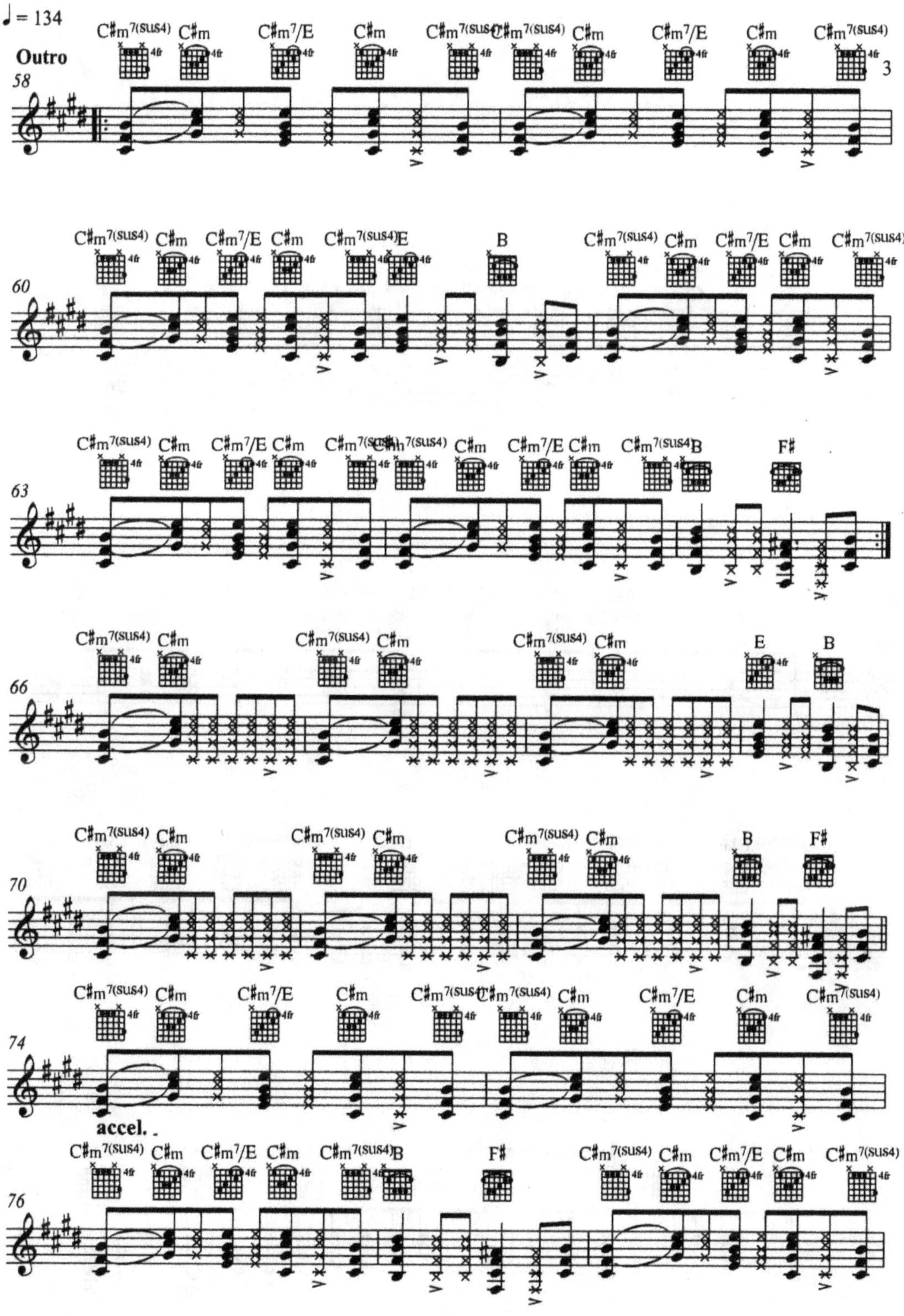
♩= 134
Outro
C♯m7(sus4)
C♯m
C♯m7/E
E
B
F♯
3
accel.

4

C♯m7(sus4) C♯m C♯m7/E C♯m C♯m7(sus4) C♯m7(sus4) C♯m C♯m7/E C♯m C♯m7(sus4) B F♯
79
C♯m7(sus4) C♯m C♯m7/E C♯m C♯m7(sus4) C♯m7(sus4) C♯m C♯m7/E C♯m C♯m7(sus4)
82
C♯m7(sus4) C♯m C♯m7/E C♯m C♯m7(sus4) E B C♯m7(sus4) C♯m C♯m7/E C♯m C♯m7(sus4)
84
C♯m7(sus4) C♯m C♯m7/E C♯m C♯m7(sus4) C♯m7(sus4) C♯m C♯m7/E C♯m C♯m7(sus4) B F♯
Fine
87
rall.

Version 02

La Belle Dame

Music by Jonathan Hale
Lyrics by John Keats

♩=124 INTRO

Acoustic Guitar

Acoustic Guitar
capoed at 2nd fret,
sounds F#min

A. Gtr.

A. Gtr. capo

VERSES 1-10

Voice

Oh what can ail thee, ga-lant knight, alone and pale-ly loi-te-ring?

A. Gtr. capo

Voice

The sedge has wit-her'd from the - lake and no-birds sing.

A. Gtr. capo

La Belle Dame

2

Get in the Sailboat

♩=93 **INTRO**

Acoustic Guitar capoed at 5th fret*

G C G

G D⁷ G C G

VERSE 1

Voice

The-re was a time when   on this old earth   I tra veled on through trou - ble and mirth.
Oh__ sinn-er friend won't you lis - ten just now   Some-one to help you, make him your vow.
We're on our way to Hea-ven a - bove, Fly - ing a - long like a hea - ven - ly dove.

G D⁷ G C G

Voice

But Je - sus came and beck-oned you see   Get in the sail - boat with me.
Make up your mind, ac - cept him my friend Get in the sail - boat with him.
Je - sus is co - ming, co - ming a - gain Get in the sail - boat with him.

CHORUS

G C G

Voice

Get in the sail - boat with Je_____ sus get in the sail_ boat with him.

REPEAT AFTER 3RD CHORUS, END SONG

D⁷ G C G

Voice

We're tra - velin' down life's ri - ver of time Get in the sail - boat with him.

*The sounding chords are C, F, G

Something to Build

Words and music by Jonathan K. Hale

♩=85 **CHORUS**

Ac. Guitar tuned min. 3rd down*

Voice, chords at sounding pitch

Some thing to build the memo ri-es___on

Some thing to keep you warm when the

night are cold and long___ oh ba-by Some-thing-to build the memo ri-es on.

VERSE 1

No-bo-dy said love was ea-sy____ But you live and_ you learn

You'll make mis - ta - kes But that's the chance you take

You can't take fi - re in your heart and not_ get bur-ned If you want

VERSE 2

on. No-bo-dy said life was e - ven___ What you give ain't what you

*C# F# B E G# C#

43

2

get

We can't take back what we___ said   Can't take back what we did_ but you

find some-times you can still for-gi-ve   What you can't for - get___

BRIDGE

How can you see in - side until you___   put a-way your pride   See what's in our hearts and_

___   see what's in   our   minds___ There's   beau - ty   that_   we   all   hold   with - in___

___   You'll   walk   much   bet - ter   now___   my___

D.C. al coda   rit. . . . .

___ friend   'Cuz you got   Some-thing-to build the memo ri - es   on.

Cold Winds

Words and Music by Jonathan K. Hale

Drop tuning to C# (C#,F#,B,E,G#,C#)
Voice staff has the sounding chords if guitar is in standard tuning

♩=112

INTRO

VERSE 1

I feel a cool breeze blow and the

whis-pe-ring wind is like drift-ing snow on a moun - ta - in

With the sun-li-ght still on my skin

And

INTERLUDE 4 BARS

45

CHORUS
F#m C#m
Voice
oh that's where I wan-na be___ if
Am Em
A. Gtr.
18
Bm rit. F#m C#m a tempo
you would on ly close your eyes then you could see what I can see And I see
Dm Am Em
20
VERSE 2 F#m E Bm
waves cras-hing on the_docks like lost hopes dashed up -
Am G Dm
23
F#m D E F#m D E F#m
on the rocks but the clouds they look so soft_ so what if we
Am F G Am F G Am
26
INTERLUDE CHORUS
fall? And I hear
30

VERSE 3
Voice
A. Gtr.
6
D E F#m
F G Am
40
BRIDGE
F#m
C#m
So let the cold winds_ wail
let the cold winds howl
Am
Em
50
Bm
E
as they fill my sails
and roll a-cross my_ bow
Dm
G
Am
54
OUTRO
D E F#m D E
And I see you walk a - way on the shore__
and I don't know why
F G Am F G
58

4

But I can't stop it any-more____

so I just wave good-bye____   oh I just wave good

bye____   oh I just wave good-bye

At This Moment

Words and Music by
Jonathan K. Hale

©1994 - 2015 Chimery Chimes

49

2

Voice

At this mo - me - nt__ she said I love you with all__ my he-art

A. Gtr.

33

Voice

but to-mor-row mor - ni - ng__ oh you won't be back for mo - re no, no more

A. Gtr.

37

INTRO 2

Voice

repeat 4 times

A. Gtr.

41

VERSE 2

Voice

Now run-ning out_ of time I could-n't read_your mind still I take all__the bla-me They

A. Gtr.

57

Voice

say that what's done is done so are you glad_you won? I'll ne-ver be the sa-me

A. Gtr.

61

50

CHORUS
16
Voice
A. Gtr.
65
INTRO 3
F#m E6 Dmaj7 E6 F#m
1.2.3.
repeat 4 times
Em D6 Cmaj7 D6 Em
81
4.
BRIDGE
D E F#m
It's hard to hold on when all hope is go - ne but
C D Em
85
97
D E D E F#m
I'm gon-na fig - th no,
C D C D Em
100
D E
I won't go do - wn
C D
104

At This Moment - J.K. Hale

4

52

This House

Words and Music by
Jonathan K. Hale

optional capo on 2nd fret

♩=122 | INTRO 1

Voice

Acoustic Guitar capo II

VERSE 1

woke up this mor-ning oh I | knew you were gone but I | dreamed last night I held you | in my arms I

know I have your pic-ture but it's___ not eno ugh this hou-se is___ not a___ home with-out your lo-ve

INTRO 2
Voice
A. Gtr.
7
7
And this
17
CHORUS 1
F♯m A E F♯m A E
house is not_ my own___ my life is not_ my own___ and I
Em G D Em G D
25
F♯m D E
can't go on_ a - lone_with - out_your lo-ve
Em C D
INTRO 3
VERSE 2
8
8
8
8
29

VERSE 2

Now when I close my eyes I realize the truth
but I dream at night I'm lying next to you
I try to play the game but it's just no use
my life is not the same it's all a ruse

VERSE 3:

Do you know what it's like to heed the call
only to find yourself taking a fall
I'm sending out a message but there's no reply
and I can't go on without you by my side

55

Castles

Words and Music by
Jonathan K. Hale

♩=86

INTRO 1

Are your cast-les in the air? Or_ do you e-ven

care? Will you stand or will you fall? Or

Voice
A. Gtr.
F♯m
C♯m
do you care at all? Cast-les in the air.
Am
Em
12
BRIDGE instrumental
A B B(sus4) B A B
C D D(sus4) D C D
15
3
INTRO 2
VERSE 2
9
19
BRIDGE instrumental
INTRO 3
VERSE 3
4
8
And
37
BRIDGE SUNG
A B B(sus4) B
all I'll ever_ be___ just crum-bles in___ my ha- nds_ is
C D D(sus4) D
59

washed in - to___ the se - a___ like cast - les___ cast - les made of

INTRO 4

sa - nd

Bright Side

Words and Music by
Jonathan K. Hale

Time is wa - sting on the bright side of to - wn

but there rea-lly ain't no rea-son for me to be fee - ling down.

Time is was - ting on the bright side of to - wn

but there rea-lly ain't no rea-son for me to be fee - ling down.

just be - cause the sun don't shine on my side of town

Bright Side

VERSE 3

Voice
61
Rain is fall - ing   on the dark side of to - wn

Voice
65
but there rea-lly ain't no rea son   for me to be fee - ling down.

Voice
69
Rain is fall - ing   on the dark side of to - wn

Voice
73
but there rea-lly ain't no rea - son   for me to be fee - ling down.

Voice
A. Gtr.
77
'Cause I'll just move__ on   I'll just move__ on

Voice
A. Gtr.
81
Yeah, I'll just move__ on   to   that bright side   of   town

Bright Side

A. Gtr. | INTRO 4 | E | G#m | F#m | 1. B B7(sus4) B | 2. B7 B(sus4) B7 E | molto rit. | 3

VERSE 2

Wind is blowing
through my window now
ain't no way of knowing
which way she's going now.
Wind is blowing
through my window now
ain't no way of knowing
which way she's going now.
Guess i'll just hold on
for a new day now.

VERSE 3

Rain is falling
on the dark side of town
but there really ain't no reason
for me to be feeling down.
Rain is falling
on the dark side of town
but there really ain't no reason
for me to be feeling down.
'Cause i'll just move on
yeah, i'll just move on
i'll just move on
to that bright side of town.

Just Cause

Words and Music by
Jonathan K. Hale

Voice (Verse 1): Just be-cause you gave up on me___ do I have to give up on you?___ And just be-cause the sun don't shi-ne___ does it mean the rain falls, too? Of

Voice (Chorus 1): all the things that I don't know___ one thing I can say for sure___ I'm still in love_ I'm still in love I'm still in love_ with you___

Just Cause

VERSE 2

Voice

8

21

BRIDGE

Voice

Just be-cause you lose the ba-ttle   does it mean you've lost the war?____

D   E   F#m   D   E   F#m

A. Gtr.

29

Voice

just be-cause you fall from the sad-dle   does it mean you'll ride no more?____

D   E   F#m   D   E   C#

A. Gtr.

33

A. Gtr.

37

VERSE 3

Voice

8

40

CHORUS 2

Voice

Of all the things that I don't know____   one thing I can say for sure____

E   F#   G#m   E   F#   G#m

A. Gtr.

48

VERSE 2:

Just because you left me behind
does it mean i won't be around?
And just because you've raised up a wall
does it mean i can't tear it down?

BRIDGE:

And just because you lose the battle
does it mean you've lost the war?
And just because you fall from the saddle
does it mean you'll ride no more?

VERSE 3:

Just because there's nothing to say
does it mean that we can't talk?
And just because i don't hold the key anymore
does it mean i can't break the lock?

CHORUS:

Of all the things that i don't know
one thing i can say for sure
I'm still in love
I'm still in love
I'm still in love with you

Train Song

Words and Music by
Jonathan K. Hale

♩=136 **INTRO 1**

1.2.3. | **4.**

I said

C#m   B   A   B   A

VERSE 1

now ... oh the time has come ... for me to be go-

C#m   B   A   B   C#m   B   A   B

ne ... but I don't wan-na go a - lone ...

C#m   B   A   B   C#m   B   A

CHORUS 1

What do you do ... when the train kee-ps roll-ing ... and you wan-na get off?

E   B   C#m   B   A   B

Voice
A. Gtr.
21
C#m B A B E B
What do you do when the rain kee-ps fall-ing
25
C#m B A B
and it just won't stop?
INTRO 2
1.2.
3.
27
C#m B A B A
And I'm
VERSE 2
30
C#m B A B C#m B A B
le-a-ving on a mid-night tra-in I'm ne-ver
34
C#m B A B C#m B A
co-ming back ne-ver co-ming back a-gain

CHORUS 2
3
Voice
10
A. Gtr.
10
38
INTRO 3
1.2.
3.
Voice
I took a
C#m B A B A
A. Gtr.
48
Voice
late night flight
to San An-ton
Looks like I'm
C#m B A B C#m B A B
A. Gtr.
51
Voice
hea-ded south
way down to Me-xi-co
C#m B A B C#m B A
A. Gtr.
55
CHORUS 3
INTRO 4
C#m B A B C#m B A
A. Gtr.
10
59

OUTRO
Voice
A. Gtr.
Oh the train keeps roll-ing down the track train keeps roll-ing down
A C#m B A B C#m B A
72
the track train keeps roll-ing down the track
B C#m B A B C#m B A
76
A C#m B A B
80
rit.
C#m B A B
83
87

Song of Solomon

Words and Music by
Jonathan K. Hale

♩=136 — INTRO 1

Acoustic Guitar

VERSE 1

Voice: A nother sleep- less night and he'd climb the ci-ty walls to see her face but

A. Gtr.: F#m / Bm / F#m / A E

Voice: light-ning nev-er strikes the same place twice un-till the sha-dows flee and the dawn bre aks

A. Gtr.: F#m / Bm / F#m / A E

PRE-CHORUS 1

Voice: So he's search-ing in the ci-ty in the streets and in the square so he'll

A. Gtr.: D E / F#m / D E / F#m

69

Voice
hold her so close ne - ver
let her go
D E F♯m E D
A. Gtr.
21
CHORUS 1
When he finds her the - re
For love is strong as death and
A E D E F♯m
24
jea - lou - sy cruel as the grave
its
D E F♯m
28
coals are coals of fi - re
the most ve-he me - nt flames
D E F♯m D D E F♯m
30

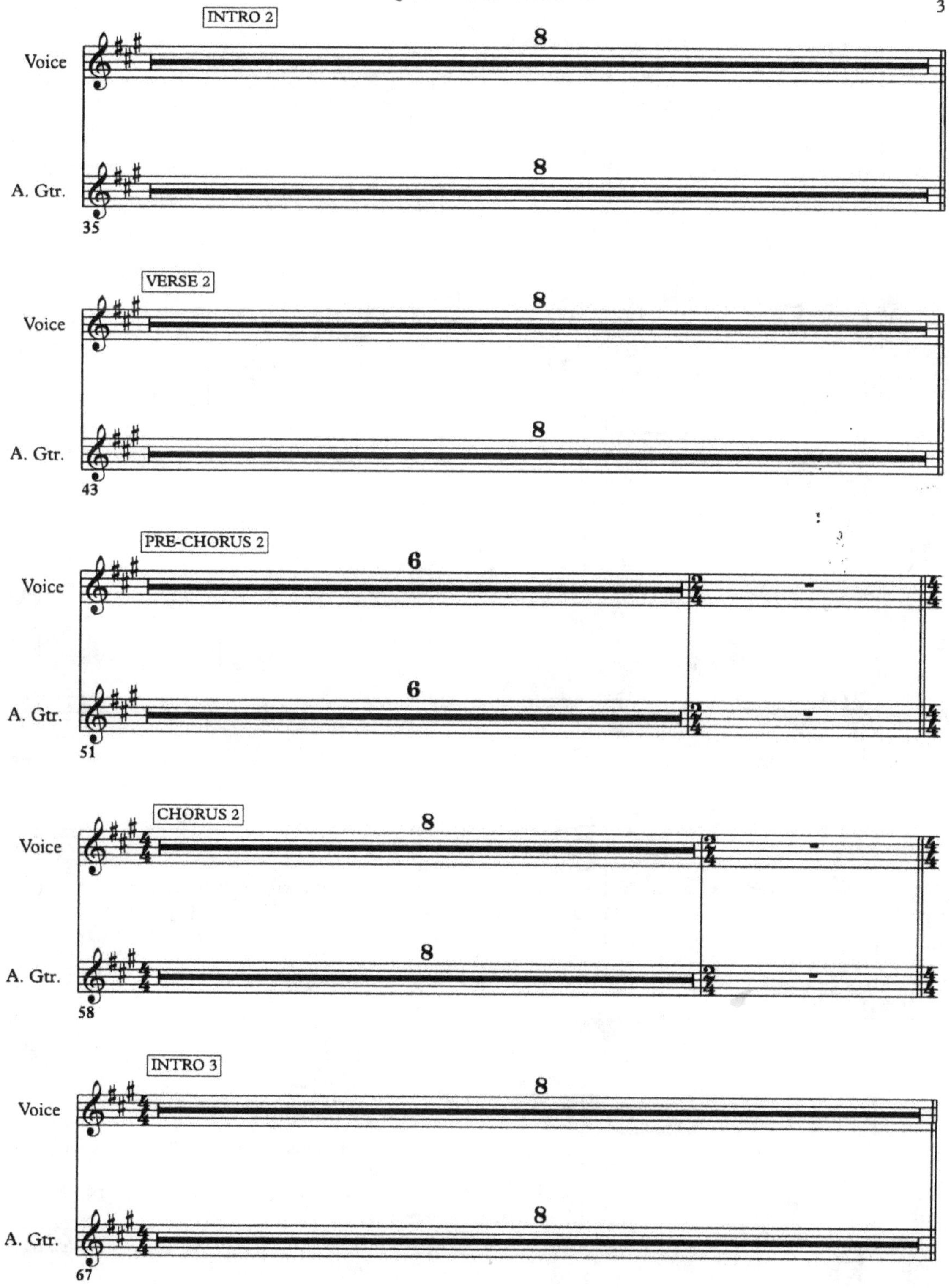
INTRO 2
Voice
A. Gtr.
35
VERSE 2
Voice
A. Gtr.
43
PRE-CHORUS 2
Voice
A. Gtr.
51
CHORUS 2
Voice
A. Gtr.
58
INTRO 3
Voice
A. Gtr.
67

4

BRIDGE

Voice: Ma-ny wa-ters can-not quench love nor can floods drown it If a man gave all he

A. Gtr. F#m | Bm | F#m | D E

75

Voice: con- tempt is all he'd get

A. Gtr. F#m | Bm | F#m | D E

79

PRE-CHORUS 3

rit. . . . . . . A tempo

5

A. Gtr. 5

83

CHORUS 3

Voice: when he finds her the - re For love is strong as death

A. Gtr. A E | D E | F#m

90

Voice: jea-lou-sy cruel as the grave its coals are coals of fi - re

A. Gtr. D E | F#m | D E F#m | D

94

Verse 1:
Another sleepless night
and he'd climb these city walls
to see her face
But lightning never strikes
the same place twice
till the shadows flee
and the dawn breaks

Pre-chorus 1:
So he's searching in the city
in the streets and in the square
he'll hold her so close
never let her go

Chorus:
When he finds her there
for love is strong as death
jealousy cruel as the grave
its coals are coals of fire
the most vehement flames

Verse 2:
She wakes from a dream
he's outside it seems
and she can hear him knocking
But she's waited too long
and now he's gone
and she's afraid she's lost him

Pre-chorus 2:
So she's searching in the city
in the streets and in the square
she'll hold him so close
never let him go

Chorus:
When she finds him there
for love is strong as death
jealousy cruel as the grave
its coals are coals of fire
the most vehement flames

Bridge:
Many waters cannot quench love
nor can floods drown it
if a man gave all he had for love
contempt is all he'd get

Pre-chorus 3:
But I'm searching in the city
in the streets and in the square
I'll hold you so close
never let you go

Chorus:
If I find you there
for love is strong as death
jealousy cruel as the grave
its coals are coals of fire
the most vehement flames

Cut Me Out

Words and music by Alvin H. Hale
arranged by Jonathan K. Hale

optional guitar tuning min 3rd down

INTRO 1

VERSE 1

you were young and lovely and your heart it beat for me : I fell in love with you darling but it end-ed bit-ter-ly. So

CHORUS 1

cut me out of your pic-ture and take it and throw it a-way cut me out of your pic-ture but I'll re-turn some day.

BRIDGE 1
(Em) C♯m (D) B (Em) C♯m (C) A
Voice
Oh...
(Em) C♯m (D) B (C(sus2)) A(sus2)
VERSE 2
CHORUS 2
BRIDGE 2
CHORUS 3
(G) E (C) A (G) E
cut me out of your pic-ture and take it and throw it a - way
(C) A (G) E (Em) C♯m (D) B (G) E
cut me out of your pic - ture but I'll re - turn some day.
BRIDGE 3
OUTRO
(Em) C♯m (D) B (Em) C♯m (C) A
I'll re - tu - rn I'll re - tu - rn oh,
(Em) C♯m (D) B (C(sus2)) A(sus2)
I'll re - tu - rn some - day.
(G) E

76

4